Gramn

Sisters

Gramma & Ginga chatting with Jimmy Kimmel

in the Kitchen

Genevieve "Gramma" Musci
and
Arlene "Ginga" Bashnett

Headline Books, Inc.
Terra Alta, WV

Gramma & her husband in 1932. Check out the old cars in the background!

In 1931 Gramma (17) & husband, Frank (18) with their daughter, Marie (Frank Alan & Sheila Lynn's mother)- not yet a year old. Gee & Frank skipped school at age 15 & 16 and got married in Oakland, Maryland as marriage at their age was not legal in the state of West Virginia. They remained married for 58 years until Frank's death.

Gramma & Ginga: Sisters in the Kitchen

by Genevieve Musci and Arlene Bashnett

To order additional copies of this book or for book publishing information, or to contact the author:

Headline Books, Inc.
P.O. Box 52
Terra Alta, WV 26764
www.headlinebooks.com

Tel: 800-570-5951
Email: mybook@headlinebooks.com

ISBN 13: 9781882658879

Ginga (13) with her brother, who was known as "Mr. Louie-the dance instructor" throughout the state of West Virginia. They tapped dance together for many years and Mr. Louie taught generations of families to dance.

PRINTED IN THE
UNITED STATES OF AMERICA

Ginga & Gramma in 1975.

This book was compiled by Gramma & Ginga's family and is dedicated to... two feisty, tell-it-like-it-is sisters, who have lived very long and full lives, raised wonderful families, and spread laughter and joy to millions throughout the world...all the while getting into a few arguments with each other—and oh yes, maybe cussing a little, too.

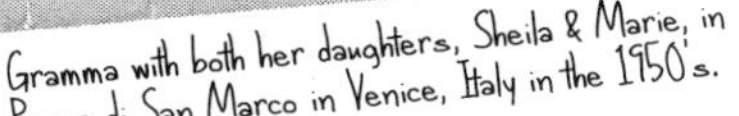

Gramma with both her daughters, Sheila & Marie, in Piazza di San Marco in Venice, Italy in the 1950's.

Gramma, age 34

Ginga coming to visit Gramma

Ginga at Festival

Ginga's Recipes

Ginga "working hard" autographing her photos to send to fans!

Ginga's Apple Cake with the Best Damn Sauce
Preheat oven to 350 degrees

Ginga 2015

3-4 large apples, chopped
2 cups sugar

Pour sugar over apples and let sit for 20 minutes or just while you prepare rest of ingredients

3 cups flour
1 ½ teaspoons baking soda
1 teaspoons salt
1 cup vegetable oil
3 eggs
1 teaspoon vanilla (the real stuff-no imitation!)
1 teaspoon nutmeg
1 teaspoon cinnamon
1 cup chopped nuts, if you like them

Combine all ingredients and pour in well greased (or sprayed) tube pan. Try not to make too much of a mess because this is one hell of a heavy batter-so have someone strong help ya! Bake at 350 degrees for 45 minutes or until tester comes out clean.

Ginga celebrating Gramma's 100th Birthday in Virginia, 2014

Best Damn Sauce:
1 ½ cups brown sugar
½ cup (1 stick) unsalted butter
¼ cup evaporated mile
1 teaspoon vanilla
½ teaspoon salt

Cook all ingredients together in small sauce pan and pour over cooled cake. Try not to eat the sauce before the cake cools!

Ginga with Gramma's great granddaughter, Genevieve

Ginga's Baked Ricotta Cheese
Preheat oven to 350

1 large 32 oz container Ricotta cheese
3 eggs, beat lightly
⅔ cup sugar
½ cup flour
1 tablespoon lemon juice (Ginga says not to go use any fake-ass lemon juice!)
3 tablespoon butter, cut into tiny bits to dot top of mixture before baking
¼ cup cinnamon sugar (mix some sugar with cinnamon)

Mix all ingredients together (except cinnamon sugar & butter) and pour into a greased 8x8 pan. Dab with butter on top and sprinkle cinnamon sugar. Bake at 350 for 40 minutes (uncovered). Enjoy!

Gramma & Ginga on the SS Constitution on their way to Italy in 1950

Ginga's Fat-ass Sour Cream Pralines

1 ½ cups sugar
1 ½ cups brown sugar
¼ teaspoon salt
¼ teaspoon baking soda
1 cup sour cream
1 tablespoon light colored corn syrup
2 tablespoon oleo (or unsalted butter)
1 teaspoon vanilla
2 cups pecans

Combine sugars, salt, soda, sour cream & corn syrup in heavy saucepan. Cook over low heat, stirring constantly until comes to soft ball (235 degrees with cooking thermometer). Remove from heat. Stir in butter, vanilla and nuts. Beat at once until its creamy and almost looses gloss. Drop in heaping tablespoons onto waxed paper or parchment paper- let stand until firm.
Try not to eat too much of this or your ass will get big!

Ginga's Beets

Gramma with her grandson, Michael & her great-grandson, Oliver.

½ cup sugar
2 teaspoon flour
½ cup water
½ vinegar
½ salt
2 tablespoons butter
2 cups cooked beets, diced (it doesn't matter how the hell you cook them- just make sure they're cooked)

Mix sugar & flour together in sauce pan. Add water and vinegar and cook on medium heat until thick, stirring constantly unless you want the damn thing to burn! Add butter and beets until the beets are heated through. Now, that doesn't mean to cook them for an hour- just until the beets are warm again- maybe 5 minutes or so.

Ginga's Dill Cucumber Salad

Ginga with Gramma's daughter, Marie

3 large cucumbers
⅓ cup vinegar
2 tablespoons water
¼ cup sugar
1 teaspoon salt
¼ teaspoon ground pepper
1 tablespoon minced dill

Peel cucumbers and slice very thin. Put them in bowl of cold water with ice cubes and chill in fridge for 1 hour. Drain and put in serving bowl. Combine all other ingredients and pour over cucumbers. Chill several hours. Drain off liquid and serve. Sprinkle lightly with dill.

Gramma & her husband, Frank with their daughter, Marie, c.1932

Ginga's Best Damn Cake Ever

1 cup nuts, chopped
2 cups sugar
2 cups flour
2 teaspoons baking soda
2 eggs
1 teaspoon vanilla
1 can crushed pineapple (undrained)
1 cup coconut

Mix by hand if you've got it in ya and bake at 350 degrees for 40-45 mins

Icing:
1 stick butter
8 oz cream cheese
1 ½ cups powdered sugar
1 teaspoon vanilla

Mix and put on cake as soon as it come out of oven. It's supposed to kinda melt down over the cake.

Gramma (10), Ginga (5) middle, with their sister, Peenie (8)

Ginga's Italian Funnel Cake

1 egg
⅔ cup milk
¼ teaspoon salt
2 tablespoons sugar
1 ⅓ cups sifted flour
¾ teaspoon baking powder
¼ cups confectioner's sugar for dusting
vegetable oil (enough for deep-frying- will vary depending how big of a pan or kettle you use) Ginga says you want oil about 2-3 inches deep

Ginga's Buttermilk Candy

Gramma's great grandson, Brandon–surprising the girls at their Senior Citizen Center during lunch & bingo! 2015

2 cups sugar
2 cups buttermilk
1 teaspoon baking soda
2 tablespoons white Karo syrup
½ stick butter
1 teaspoon vanilla
1 cup pecans
Candy thermometer

Cook first five ingredients to 235 degrees. Cool and add vanilla & pecans. Beat mixture and drop on wax paper (or parchment paper) while still soft. Share with friends!

Ginga's Christmas Wreaths

Gramma's great granddaughters, Ava & Grace visiting

1 stick butter
40 large marshmallows
2-3 tablespoons of green food coloring
4 cups corn flakes

Melt stick of butter in large pan. Add 40 marshmallows and mix until melted. Add in enough green food coloring to your liking. Mix in corn flakes and drop teaspoonfuls on wax paper.

Ginga's Fat-ass Chocolate Fudge

3 cup sugar
1 envelope unflavored gelatine
1 cup milk
½ cup light corn syrup
4 squares (4 oz) unsweetened chocolate
1 ¼ cups butter
2 teaspoon vanilla extract
1 cup walnuts, coarsely chopped

Butter an 8 x 8 x 2 inch pan or Pyrex glass dish

In a small sauce pan, mix sugar with gelatin. Add milk, corn syrup, chocolate and butter.

Cook over medium heat stirring frequently until mixture makes a little ball that you can flatten with your finger when dropped in cold water. (Soft ball stage) If you're all fancy and you have a cooking thermometer- that's 235 degrees F.

Remove from heat and pour into a large mixing bowl. Stir in vanilla and cool 30 minutes.

Beat with wooden spoon until it thickens. Stir in nuts and spread into pan. Let cool and cut into squares. Make sure you share this otherwise you'll soon have a fat ass!

Ginga having a blast celebrating her 96th Birthday in Virginia!

Paul, Gramma's grandson, and his wife, Gail, celebrating the holidays with Ginga. 2015

Ginga's favorite Carrot Walnut Raisin Cake

2 ½ cups walnuts, divided (save the 1/2 c large pieces for decorating cake)
1 ¼ cups sifted flour
1 teaspoon salt
1 teaspoon baking soda
1 teaspoon baking powder
3 eggs
1 cup sugar
1 cup vegetable oil
3 cups grated carrots
1 ½ cups raisins
Cream cheese frosting

Gramma celebrating her 90th Birthday with her five grandchildren, Mike, David, Paul, Frank Alan & Sheila Lynn

Chop the 2 cups walnuts coarsely and remember to keep the other 1/2 c whole for decorating cake. Sift flour with salt, soda & baking powder. Beat eggs; beat in sugar & oil. Add flour mixture and mix until smooth. Stir in carrots, raisins, and chopped nuts.

Turn into well greased 10-inch tube pan. If pan has a removable bottom- sit pan on sheet of aluminum foil, cupping edges up around pan so it doesn't leak out all over your damn oven.

Bake at 350 degrees for 60-65 mins or until cake tests done. Cool in pan. When cake is cooled, remove it from pan and spread cream cheese frosting on top. Decorate with nuts. Cake can be frozen. Makes one 10-inch cake.

Gramma & Ginga living it up in Italy c.1980

Cream cheese frosting:

1 (8oz) package cream cheese, at room temp
½ cup soft butter
3 cup sifted confectioner's sugar
1 teaspoon vanilla or brandy :)

Cream the cheese together with soft butter. Gradually beat in sifted sugar. Blend in vanilla or brandy! Enjoy!

Ginga's Favorite Cookie Bars

Gramma & Ginga showing off gifts they received from their kind fans in Kuwait!

1 cup Graham crackers
1 stick butter, melted

Stir together and line pan. Ginga doesn't remember what size pan she used- so wing it!

1 cup chocolate chips (don't matter what kind)
1 cup chopped nuts (yeah, you got it- any kind ya like)
1 cup coconut (Ginga thinks she used sweetened coconut)
1 cup condensed milk (now you don't think Ginga remembers what size can...so wing this too!)

Pour mixture over graham crackers and bake at 350 degrees for about 25-30 minutes.
These will make your ass big too- so share them with your neighbors!

Ginga's Honey Bunny Fruit Drops

Preheat oven to 350 degrees

½ cup each of chopped candied fruits,
chopped candied cherries, raisins, and chopped pecans
¼ cup bourbon (there Ginga goes again!)
½ cup packed brown sugar
¼ cup honey
½ cup butter or margarine
2 eggs
2 ¾ cup flour
½ teaspoon baking soda
1 teaspoon cinnamon
½ teaspoon ground nutmeg
¼ teaspoon baking powder
¼ cup sour cream

Sheila Lynn having fun with G&G at the West Virginia Italian Heritage Festival Luncheon, 2015

Combine fruits, nuts and bourbon. Cover and let stand 1 hour. In mixing bowl combine sugar, honey & butter. Beat in eggs.
Mix dry ingredients. Add to honey mixture. Mix in fruit. Drop by teaspoons onto greased cookie sheet. Bake in 350 degree oven 10-12 minutes. Cool on wire rack. Should make about 5 dozen cookies.

Ginga's Favorite Ice Box Cookies

Ginga goofing off with Gramma's great grandson, Christian!

2 cup brown sugar
1 cup margarine, melted
2 eggs, beaten
4 cup flour
1 teaspoon salt
1 teaspoon baking soda
½ cup cherries, chopped
½ cup walnuts, chopped

Mix together all ingredients and roll in wax paper. (Ginga says it makes 4 rolls). Store in refrigerator until firm. Can be kept in fridge about 4 days. May also be frozen.
Slice ¼ inches thick and bake 20 minutes at 325 degrees.

Ginga's Fruit Cocktail Cake

The gals excited to see Frank Alan & Sheila Lynn. They know they're going to have some fun

1 ½ cups sugar
2 cups flour
2 teaspoon baking soda
2 cups fruit cocktail
2 eggs

Mix sugar and egg. Add soda and flour then the fruit cocktail. Mix well. Bake in baking 8x8 pan for 35-45 minutes at 350 degrees.

Frost while hot with:

1 ½ cup sugar
1 cup cream
¼ lb or 1 stick of oleo
½ teaspoon vanilla

Boil 2 mins and pour on cake while hot.

Ginga's Glazed Lemon Cake
Preheat oven to 350

Ginga showing off her new sticker! Go Ginga!

2 ¾ cup flour
1/2 c oil
2 teaspoon baking powder
3 eggs
½ cup milk
5 tablespoon fresh lemon juice
1 cup sugar
½ teaspoon salt
1 cup vanilla yogurt
1 teaspoon vanilla

Glaze:
1 ½ cup confectioner's sugar
3 tablespoons fresh lemon juice (more if glaze does not drizzle)

Mix all ingredients and pour into a 9x5 inch pan which has been sprayed with Pam and lined with parchment paper & sprayed again if you want the damn cake to come out.

Bake for about 55-60 minutes or until tester comes out clean.
Remove cake from pan and let cool. When cool, drizzle glaze over cake!

Ginga's Glossy Chocolate Frosting

Ginga with Frank Alan and his wife, Chelsea

½ cup sugar
2 tablespoons cornstarch
½ cup boiling water
1 square (1oz) chocolate, cut into pieces
¼ teaspoon salt
2 tablespoons butter, unsalted
1 teaspoon vanilla

In 1 quart saucepan combine sugar & cornstarch. Then stir in water, chocolate & salt. Cook over medium heat until mixture thickens, stirring frequently. Remove from heat. Stir in butter & vanilla.
Enough to frost two 9" cake layers.

The gals with their dear friend, Father Alfred

Ginga with her son, Allen

Ginga's Lemon Treat
Preheat oven to 350 degrees

1 stick butter, unsalted
2- 5.1 oz boxes instant lemon pudding
½ cup pecans, chopped
3 c vitamin D milk
1 cup flour
mandarin orange slices for garnish
1 8oz cream cheese
1 cup powdered sugar
8oz of cool whip

Mix together 1 stick butter with pecans & flour. Pat mixture into bottom of 9x12 inch pan and bake for 15 mins

Mix together cream cheese with sugar and beat in 1/2 cool whip and spread on cooled crust

Lastly, mix together instant Lemon Pudding with milk- beat for 2 minutes

Spread lemon mixture over 2nd layer & spread remaining cool whip on top & garnish with oranges.

Ginga's Little Spinach Balls
Preheat oven to 350 degrees

G&G came out to meet Frank Alan after his grueling 2,500 mile bike race across the country. He rode from California to Clarksburg, WV & raised over $100,000 for a young man named Ryan, who was attached and left in a vegetative state

2 package frozen chopped spinach, drained well
5 eggs, beaten
2 large onions, chopped fine
¾ cup butter, melted
½ cup Parmesan cheese
1 tablespoon garlic, minced
½ teaspoon thyme
½ teaspoon cayenne pepper
1 tablespoon accent
2 cups bread crumbs

(thyme, cayenne & Accent spice are optional). I was gonna say- I can't' see Ginga cookin' with Thyme!!! Maybe oregano- but not Thyme!

Cook spinach as directed. Mix together all ingredients into well drained spinach. Mold into small balls and bake at 350 degrees for 20 minutes or until brown.

Christian getting some G&G love!

Ginga's Mocha Pecan Balls
Preheat oven to 375

2 sticks unsalted butter
½ cup sugar
2 teaspoon vanilla
1 tablespoon instant espresso powder
¼ cup unsweetened coco powder
¾ teaspoon salt
1 ¾ cups flour
2 cups finely chopped pecans
confectioners sugar for rolling balls in

Cream the butter and sugar until fluffy. Add vanilla, espresso, cocoa & salt. Next, add flour and beat until combined. Add pecans and let batter rest for 1 hours in refrigerator. **Ginga used to call their refrigerator the "ice-box" because once a week the "Ice man" would come with a giant brick of ice and that's what would keep their food cold. Lastly, roll into balls and bake at 375 degrees for 12-15 minutes. Let cool for 5 minutes and roll balls in powdered sugar.

Checks out Gramma's giant Amalfi Coast lemons!

Gramma's First Grade photo

Gramma's Recipes

Gramma's 95th birthday

Gramma's "Candy"

Gramma & her great granddaughter, Audrey, at her First Holy Communion, Holy Trinity Catholic Church, Georgetown

3 cups sugar
1 gelatin package
1 cups milk
½ white Karo syrup
3 bars unsweetened Baker's chocolate
2 ½ sticks butter
1 cup nuts, chopped

Cook all these ingredients in sauce pan for 15-20 minutes
Then add vanilla. Cool for 30 minutes and then beat and add nuts. Pour mixture into lined 8" square pan and let cool into fudge; cut into pieces and enjoy! You may also drop spoonfuls of candy onto waxed paper

---

Gramma's "Tiela" of "Diela" (whatever she calls it!)

Gramma with her dear friend and neighbor, Diana, at Saint James The Apostle Catholic Church, Clarksburg, West Virginia 2016

4 tablespoons oil
2 medium squash
½ teaspoon salt
¼ teaspoon garlic powder
1 small yellow or white onion
½ cup seasoned bread crumbs
Small jalapeño pepper- optional
½-1 cup Parmesan cheese, grated

Wash and slice squash, let sit in colander, sprinkle with salt.

Beginning with onion, chop up into small pieces and sauté in hot oil about 10 minutes. Add sliced squash to onions and cook till tender but not mushy (another 10 minutes). Finely chop hot pepper and add (optional) unless you don't like hot-ass stuff!

Once sautéed and tender, sprinkle in bread crumbs and Parmesan cheese. So good you'll be thanking Gramma on FB!

Gramma's *Naughty Banana Nut Bread
Preheat oven to 350

1 ½ cup flour
1 cup sugar
1 ½ teaspoon baking soda
½ teaspoon salt
1 egg
3 tablespoons milk (*if your feeling naughty- use 3 tablespoons Rum or cooking sherry!)
½ cup veg oil
2 teaspoon vanilla
½ cup nuts, chopped
3 ripe bananas, mashed

Out to dinner at Twin Oaks with her three grandchildren, Frank, Sheila & Paul

Stir together all dry ingredients. Beat egg and mix in oil and eggs. Mix with flour and add bananas, vanilla and nuts. Pour into greased and floured loaf pan and bake for approximately 1 hour depending on your oven.

Gramma's Barbecue Sause

1 chopped onion
2 tablespoon vinegar
2 tablespoon Worchestershire Sause
1 teaspoon salt
½ teaspoon black pepper
1 teaspoon chili powder
¾ cup Ketchup
¾ cup water
½ cup brown sugar

Gramma with her wonderful friends, Maryk & Dody, during a trip to the Amalfi Coast, Italy

Mix all ingredients together and brush on spare ribs or chicken or whatever you're cooking! So damn good- Enjoy!

Gramma with daughter, Marie & great granddaughters, twins-Ava & Grace and Christian (gramma's great grandson)

Gramma's Chili

2 lbs ground beef
1 onion, chopped
2 garlic cloves, minced
1 green pepper, chopped
1 red pepper, chopped
2 tablespoons Chili powder
1 tablespoon Cayenne pepper
4 tablespoons oil
1 28oz can stewed tomatoes, dices
1 8oz can tomato paste
1 8oz can tomato paste (empty) filled with water

In medium pot, add oil and cook onion and peppers until tender- about 10 minutes. Add meat and brown. Add rest of ingredients, cover and bring to slow boil. Reduce heat and simmer for 30 mins.

Gramma's Corn Dish
Preheat oven to 350 degrees

1 - 14.5 oz can reg corn
1 - 14.5 oz can creamed corn
1 egg, slightly beaten
⅓ cup dry bread crumbs
½ cup sour cream
Salt & pepper to taste
parsley

Mix all ingredients together and pour into casserole dish. Bake for 40 minutes at 350 degrees.

Gramma with her daughters, Marie & Sheila c.1940

Gramma's Easter Bread from Aunt Rosie
Preheat oven to 350 degrees

G&G feasting at T&L Hotdogs!

5 small cakes of yeast or 5 pkgs fast rising yeast
3 tablespoons vanilla
4 ½ cups sugar
½ lb butter, softened
5 large eggs, beaten
1 ⅓ teaspoons salt
1 quart warm milk
Few drops of yellow food coloring

If using cakes of yeast, measure water so liquid does not exceed more than 4 cups measure. Gramma has found this to be the best practice. We listen to Gramma!

Mix all ingredients- Let rise.
Form dough into 2 loaves and place in well greased pans.
Beat another egg & brush on top of loaves, sprinkle with sugar and bake 30-45 mins. Gramma says this is a classic! Recipe given to her by Aunt Rosie, who was big and fat and a great cook & baker!

Gramma's Famous Chocolate Frosting

Gramma & Ginga have had enough of this 'Sh*%.' G&G for Pres & VP!

½ cup shortening
1 egg
½ cup cocoa
¼ teaspoon salt
4 cups confectioners sugar
1 teaspoon vanilla
⅓ cup milk

Blend shortening, egg, cocoa & salt. Add sugar alternately with milk and vanilla, mixing until smooth. Add more sugar to thicken frosting if necessary.

This frosts two 8-9 inch layers or one 9x13 inch cake.

Gramma's Fried Smelts

G&G on the Senior Citizen bus during the 2015 West Virginia Italian Heritage Festival

3 dozen smelts
2 cups flour
Salt to taste
½ teaspoon pepper
½ teaspoon garlic powder
Enough veg oil to fill 3 inches of frying pan
Paper or plastic bag for shaking

Buy smelts at local grocery store. You may need to order them ahead of time

Wash and clean the little fish under cold water. Gramma splits them open with a knife and clears out intestinal track like you do with shrimp. Dry with paper towels

Place flour in paper or plastic zip lock bag, add garlic powder, pepper, add 6-7 smelts, shake to coat with flour, shake off excess and drop into hot oil and let fry for 2-3 mins or until slightly browned. Time may vary depending on how hot oil is.
Drain on paper towels and salt to taste. Enjoy!

The gals together celebrating the holidays in Virginia with their grandchildren

Gramma's Roasted Potatoes & Onions
Preheat oven to 450

2 lbs potatoes, cut into bite size chunks
1 onion, chopped
Salt to taste
Pepper
1/3 c oil

In large bowl, add all ingredients and toss to thoroughly coat. On roasting pan, arrange potatoes & onions and bake uncovered stirring occasionally for about 40 minutes until potatoes are golden brown and crispy.

Gramma's Fruit Cookies
Preheat over to 350 degrees

G&G having breakfast in Virginia and getting ready for their trip home to Clarksburg, WV

1 lb butter
3 eggs
1 lb white raisins
1 lb candied cherries
1 cup coconut, moist
1 teaspoon baking soda
1 lb brown sugar

3 tablespoons sweet milk- whatever the hell that is! (sweetened condensed milk) or Bourbon (Gramma!! we caught ya!!!) instead of milk... We can't believe what we just read!! Holy hell! Ginga must have given you this recipe! ;)

1 lb candied pineapple
1 lb nuts, chopped (any kind you like)
4 cups flour
1 teaspoon vanilla

Cut up fruit into little pieces. In a "giant-ass" bowl, mix brown sugar and butter. Mix until nice and creamy and add BOURBON! Whoop whoop!! Beat in eggs, then add flour, soda, nuts fruit & coconut.

Gramma says to Mix By Hand! Drop by tablespoons on cookie sheet. (Nowadays, we like to line the cookie sheet with parchment paper to make clean up easier- but it's not necessary). Gramma sure as hell did not use parchment paper! Bake in 350 degree oven for only 10 minutes, she says! That seems too short a time but if she was sippin' the Bourbon- maybe she cut the baking time short! ha!

Frank taking a selfie with the gals!

G&G posing for a photo in Kroger "1-2-3 Sex!"

Gramma's Honey Butter Italian Toast

½ cup butter, at room temp
½ cup honey
¼ teaspoon vanilla extract
½ teaspoon cinnamon

In small bowl mix all ingredients until creamy. Slice Italian bread and toast. While bread is warm, slather on Honey Butter and enjoy! Gramma used to make this for all the grandchildren when we were little.

Gramma & Ginga celebrating Frank's arrival into Clarksburg, WV after riding 2500 miles from California on his bike!

Gramma's Italian meat Sauce

1 - Pork neck bone
Salt to taste (start with 1 tsp)
1 teaspoon Garlic powder
2 small 8 oz cans tomato paste
2 - large 28 oz can of stewed tomatoes
1 - can crushed tomatoes
Water to cover pork neck

Cut and trim pork neck of excessive fat, wash with cold water and pat dry with paper towels. Using very large kettle, place pork neck in kettle and turn on heat to medium. Sprinkle with 1 teaspoon salt &1 teaspoon garlic powder & cook pork neck until no pink remains- should be white in color when cooked.

Add tomato paste, 2 cans tomatoes & stir. Add enough cold water to cover pork and then add 1 can crushed tomatoes and let cook for 1 hour. Gramma skims the fat from top of sauce. Taste and if more salt is needed- add to your taste.

Gramma's Italian Sausage & Potatoes

Buy 5 lbs of Italian sausage from your favorite Italian sausage maker or from your local grocery store.

2-lbs of potatoes (can be any kind), washed & cut into ½-1" pieces

Heat oven to 375 degrees, after 20 minutes, change to 350 degrees

½ cup water
4 tablespoons vegetable oil
Salt to taste
Pepper to taste
Shallow Sheet pan (12"x18"X1")

Gramma cuts up sausage into ½-1" pieces and places them on her sheet pan.
Then she adds bite-size potatoes to the sausage, ½ cups water to pan to help make "juice" as sausage bakes.

Add salt & pepper to taste- be careful not to add too much salt as sausage has salt in it already. She tries to aim her salt at the potatoes. Last she adds about 4 tablespoons of oil.

Carefully place pan in middle of preheated oven and bake for 20 minutes. Open oven and stir potatoes & sausage around so that all sides brown. Turn oven temp down to 350 degrees and cook another 20 minutes or so until potatoes are browned and sausage appears to be cooked through. Can be served immediately or after cooled to room temp. This is the first thing to disappear on Christmas Eve!

The gals waving to their friend Jim who sent them candy from Mississippi!

Gramma's Jelly & Nut Cookies

Preheat oven to 350 degrees

The gals visiting their favorite hair salon in Virginia, 2015

2 cups shortening
1 cup brown sugar
2 egg yolks (save egg whites in separate bowl)
2 teaspoon vanilla
4 cups flour
2 cups nuts, chopped
1 ½ cups of strawberry jelly or jam (we decided jam is better!)
pinch salt

Mix all ingredients together and shape into 1 inch balls. Roll in beaten egg whites and then in chopped nuts. Bake for 12-14 mins (or until they are slightly brown). Gramma forgot to write down how long you bake these little guys so we tried 12 mins with my oven and they turned out well. You may need to bake them a little longer.

Gramma's One-Step Pound Cake

Gramma with her daughter, Marie, back in 1960

Preheat oven to 325 degrees

2 ¼ cups all purpose flour
2 cups sugar
1 teaspoon almond extract
½ teaspoon salt
½ teaspoon baking soda
1 cup sour cream
1 cup butter, softened
1 teaspoon vanilla
3 eggs

Generously grease & lightly flour a flute or tube pan. In large bowl, blend sour cream, butter, extract, vanilla & eggs at low speed. Add flour, sugar, salt & baking soda until moistened and then beat 3 minutes. Pour batter into prepared pan. Bake in preheated oven for 55-60 minutes or until toothpick comes out clean. Cool 15 minutes and invert onto serving plate. After cooled completely sprinkle with powdered sugar if you so desire.

Gramma's Pasta with Shrimp & Peppers

1-1 1/2 lb of linguine or spaghetti (actually any kind of pasta will work- sometimes Gramma used rigatoni when she had guests and she didn't want all the sauce to be flicked around all over her kitchen furniture- rigatoni is easier to navigate with a fork than the long unwieldy strands of linguine or spaghetti!)...ha! It's all about keeping things clean!

1 - 1 ½ cups olive oil
1 stick butter
4 colorful bell peppers (red, green, yellow, orange), sliced
2 cloves garlic
4 long green onions, chopped(both white & green parts)
Juice of ½ lemon
½ large 15oz bottle low sodium soy sauce
1- 2 lb bag 3-40 count frozen cooked Shrimp (thaw first- put in fridge at least I day before). You can use fresh uncooked unshelled shrimp which will add even more flavor but Gramma didn't like these because you have to de-shell them in your pasta plate and it was too much work for her (and it was messy and Gramma doesn't like anything that's messy!) More of a chance for the buttery sauce to flick on her nice blouse ;) You can use any size shrimp you like, too! Actually, once she forgot the shrimp altogether and did we hear "Aww Bullshit!" The pasta was still good with the shrimp omitted- so if you want to save money - make it without the shrimp- just don't tell Gramma!

In a "large-ass' skillet or frying pan- pour in oil & melt butter over medium heat. Add chopped long green onion parts and stir around for a few minutes (3 minutes is fine). Add in all four colorful bell peppers (all sliced) and let them cook for 5 minutes till they're not so crispy anymore. Add in chopped garlic, soy sauce, & lemon juice, mix and let simmer all together another 5 minutes on medium heat. Add thawed (already cooked) shrimp and stir to warm through & coat with sauce- don't let cook too long otherwise shrimp will get tough.

While making sauce start boiling your water for the pasta in a large pot with 1 teaspoon salt. Add pasta & cook. When your pasta is al dente (still firm when you bite it) drain it and add to pot of sauce (if you have room). If you don't have a pan big enough for both- find yourself a "giant-ass" serving bowl and add your pasta & sauce to the bowl and mix it all up.

Gramma's Peanut Butter Fudge

Gramma showing off another Birthday bouquet of fruit!

2 cup sugar
¼ cup unsulphured molasses
¼ cup butter
½ cup milk
¼ teaspoon salt
1 teaspoon vanilla
1 cup peanut butter

In a 3 quart pan, mix sugar, molasses butter milk and salt. Stir over low heat until sugar is dissolved. Cook till mixture reaches 236 degrees. You can test by dropping a small amount of syrup in cold water- it will form a soft ball.

Remove from heat and cool until slightly warm (about 110 degree). Add vanilla & peanut butter. Beat candy until it begins to thicken and loses its gloss. Pour into buttered 8x8x2-inch pan. After set, cut into squares.

Gramma's Pickled eggs in Beet juice

1 dozen eggs - any size
2-3 large jars pickled beets
1 cup vinegar
Hard boil 1 dozen eggs

Gramma posing with her Birthday flowers, 2015

Place eggs in bottom of large pan and cover with water by 1 inch. Turn on heat to high and bring to boil. Cover with lid and turn off heat as soon as water comes to a boil- let sit covered for 17 minutes.

Pour off hot water and run cold water over eggs to cool a bit, drain and peel when they have cooled enough to handle.

Place hard boiled eggs in deep enough container that will allow beet juice to cover.

Drain & keep juice from 2-3 large jars of pickled beets. Pour juice into sauce pan & add 1 cup of vinegar & heat to boil. Pour hot mixture over eggs, add in sliced beets and chill in fridge.

Gramma's Pineapple Dessert

The gals at their Harrison County Senior Citizen Center in 2014

1½ - 8 oz Lg Philadelphia Cream Cheese
1 - 20 oz can of pineapple pieces
1 - 20 oz can of pineapple, crushed
1 - 15oz can of mandarin oranges
1 small 0.3 oz box of orange Jello
1 regular 8oz container cool whip

In large bowl let cream cheese come to room temperature. Mix in orange Jello. Cream together.
Mix in cool whip and blend well. Drain fruit, add to mixture and mix well. Then spoon into serving dish and garnish with mandarin orange segments. Chill before serving.

Gramma's Pumpkin Bread

Preheat oven to 350

Gramma buying her favorite olives at her local Italian grocery store

3 cups sugar
1 cup oil
3 eggs
3 cups flour
½ teaspoon baking powder
1 teaspoon baking soda
1 teaspoon nutmeg
1 teaspoon clove
1 teaspoon cinnamon
½ teaspoon salt
2 cups pumpkin

Blend sugar and oil. Add beaten eggs one at a time. Stir dry ingredients together with whisk and add to creamed mixture and pumpkin. Bake in 2 well greased loaf pans at 350 degrees for 75 minutes.

Gramma's Potato salad

Warning! There are no exact measurement but this is well worth trying! It makes a boat load of potatoes salad ;)

Jason giving his great grandma a rose just before they board their flight to Italy in celebration of her 100th Birthday!

6-7 large (baking) potatoes
2 - 30oz jars of Miracle whip (may not use all)
2 - 16oz jars of sweet gherkin pickles, cut into little pieces
18 hard boiled eggs, cut into small pieces
1 - teaspoon of yellow mustard
Salt to taste
1 small 4oz jar of pimentos, chopped
Paprika to decorate top of potato salad

Wash & place 6-7 large potatoes (like you'd use for a baked potato) in a big pot and cover with cold water. Bring water to boil and cook potatoes until knife inserted into center finds the potato tender. May take about 20-30 mins or so. (Gramma does not like "crunchy" potatoes in her potato salad).
Once potatoes are tender, drain and when cooled, peel them and cut them into ½" chunks, set aside.
Place cut up potatoes in mixing bowl and add chopped eggs. Add some salt and mix. Add all other ingredient (except Miracle Whip) and combine with a little more salt, if needed. Add 1 jar Miracle Whip and mix well...you may need to add ½-¾ of second jar. Mix well and chill. Sprinkle paprika on top to decorate.

Gramma's Ranch Veggie Salad

Gramma with her youngest great grandson, Christian

1 package frozen peas
1 head cauliflower, cut in bite size pieces
1 head of broccoli, cut into little florets
1 can water chestnuts, drained
1½-2 cup Hellmans Mayonnaise
1 cup sour cream
1 package Hidden Ranch Herb dressing
Garlic salt to taste

Mix all and marinate a few hours or overnight.

Gramma's Snow Ball Cookies
Preheat oven to 325 degrees

You'll always find the gals shopping at Kroger!

6 tablespoons powdered sugar
 + 2 cups powdered sugar in plastic bag to shake
1¼ cup flour
1/2 lb unsalted butter (2 sticks)
2 teaspoons vanilla
1 cup nuts, chopped

Mix all ingredients except the 2 cups powdered sugar in bag.
Roll into 1 inch balls and place on cookie sheet lined with parchment paper.
Bake for 20-25 minutes
Let cool and drop in bag with powdered sugar and shake to coat.
Try not to eat them all because Gramma says you'll get a fat ass!

Gramma's Strawberry Bread
Preheat oven to 350

The gals at their Senior Center

2- 10 oz packages frozen
 strawberries, thawed
4 eggs
1¼ cups veg oil
3 cups flour
2 cups sugar
3 teaspoons baking soda
3 teaspoons cinnamon
1 teaspoon salt
1 cup nuts, chopped

In large bowl mix strawberries, eggs & oil. Combine all dry ingredients and add to strawberry mixture. Pour into 2 greased and floured loaf pans and back at 350 for 1 hour. Enjoy!

Genevieve, known as "Gee" to most of her friends and "Gramma" by millions of her fans on Facebook and Youtube, was born on March 21, 1914, in Adamston, West Virginia. Soon after, her family moved to Clarksburg, WV. She grew up in North View with her parents, Maria Theresa Audia Buttafusco and Salvatore Buttafusco, one brother, Louie, and two sisters, Floranda and Arlene (Ginga).

Genevieve skipped school to get married to Frank Musci when she was fifteen and he was sixteen. They were married for 58 years until Frank passed in 1988. Genevieve had two daughters, the late Marie Romano Fumich and the late Sheila Harris. Gee enjoys spending time with her many grandchildren and great-grandchildren and her sister, Arlene ("Ginga").

Today at 102, she is proud to say that she has made 40 trips to Italy. The last trip was in celebration of her 100th Birthday! Gee also enjoys seeing her many friends at St. James Catholic Church and paying her respects to old friends at her local funeral homes.

If you visit Clarksburg, WV you will probably run into her and her "side kick" Ginga, taking photos with their new Facebook fans at their local grocery store or out at their favorite restaurant.

Arlene Cody Bashnett, was born on February 4, 1919 to Maria Theresa (Audia) & Salvatore Buttafusco of San Giovanni in Fiore, Italy. She was born and raised on Williams Avenue in Clarksburg, WV.

As a young girl, Ginga danced professionally with her brother, a dance instructor, know as "Mr. Louie" to most everyone in Harrison County, West Virginia.

Today, at 97, Arlene continues to enjoy a very full life. She lives with her son, Allen, his wife, and her grandson.

Ginga has been a volunteer at the United Hospital Center and the Veterans Hospital for nearly 30 years where she delivers get-well cards and poses for photos with her fans. She loves to spend time with her family, visit her many friends in West Virginia and Virginia, have lunch & play bingo at the Harrison County Senior Center, & eat chocolate candy!

Today, she is best known for making millions laugh as "Gramma's" hilarious sidekick—"Ginga" on Facebook & Youtube and is often recognized for her appearances on *The Jimmy Kimmel Show*.